Volume 11
I Know the Scriptures Are True

A year's worth of simple messages that can be given during church or family home evening

Volume 11
I Know the Scriptures Are True

**A year's worth of simple messages
that can be given during church
or family home evening**

**by Heidi Doxey
Illustrated by Glenn Harmon**

**CFI
Springville, Utah**

ISBN: 978-1-59955-430-3

Published by CFI,
an imprint of Cedar Fort, Inc.
2373 W. 700 S, Springville, Utah, 84663
www.cedarfort.com

Cover design by Danie Romrell
Cover design © 2010 by Lyle Mortimer
Edited and typeset by Megan E. Welton

Printed in the United States of America
10 9 8 7 6 5 4 3 2 1

Printed on acid-free paper

To my dad for teaching me about the gospel,
big dreams, and especially the "R" word.
I love you, Papa.

Contents

Contents

Introduction

This year in Primary, we are learning all about the scriptures. The theme is, "I Know the Scriptures Are True." When you think about the stories in the scriptures and learn to apply them to your life, you will see that Heavenly Father has prepared many important messages for us in the scriptures. Our job is to find those messages so we can feel his love. This book is a great resource when you need to write a talk for Primary—especially at the last minute—but it can also be used in family home evenings or for individual study. Discussing the principles in this book with your family will bring you all closer and teach you to apply the gospel directly to your lives. Each talk in this book includes five different elements: a story, a scripture, a visual aid, a list of suggested illustrations, and a discussion question.

Story

The scriptures contain a wealth of information from Heavenly Father, but in order to access the teachings and truths they contain, we need to know how to apply their lessons to our own experience here on earth. This is a necessary skill for salvation and one your children can learn early. The stories in this book come from the scriptures and from real life. As you read them, encourage your children to think of other stories from the scriptures and their own lives that incorporate the topics in the lesson. Nephi tells us that we need to "liken all scriptures unto us" and that this will benefit us and help us to learn from them (1 Nephi 19:23).

Visual Aid

In addition to a story, each talk includes a reference to a visual aid from the Gospel Art Picture Kit (GAK) or Gospel Art Book (GAB). Both are available online and can be excellent helpers. Though the Gospel Art Picture Kit has been discontinued by church distribution, I included it here for those who have not yet replaced their copy with a Gospel Art Book. However, most of the pictures are repeated in the two resources, so you should have no trouble finding a picture that will coordinate with the story. If you wish to purchase your own copy of the Gospel Art

Book, it is available through church distribution. Another option is to personalize a talk by having your children illustrate it themselves.

List of Illustrations

With each talk you will find a list of suggested illustrations that complement the story. This is especially useful for children who are too young to read the talk themselves. By having your children color their own pictures of the things discussed in the talk, you will help them remember the concepts they learned as you encourage them to share their talents. Some of these illustrations repeat in later talks, so you may want to keep your pictures handy to use again later. In this way you and your family can build your own personal art kit to use in family home evening and other settings. In years to come, this will be a treasured resource and will bring back lots of good memories.

Thought Question

Finally, each talk includes a thought question. These questions are specifically geared toward older children and teenagers, though with a little parental prompting, they can also be appropriate for young children. I hope these questions will help you to include your whole family in the lessons. They can be a great way to spark discussion and delve a little deeper into the implications of the doctrine being discussed. Make sure you let your children have a chance to express their thoughts. You may be surprised by how much they have already learned about the gospel.

I hope you will enjoy this book and the beautiful illustrations by Glenn Harmon. I am so grateful for my own family and the lessons they have taught me about the gospel. I know that we will all find strength and comfort in the scriptures as we learn more about them this year.

Chapter 1

Heavenly Father Speaks to Us through the Scriptures

—2 Nephi 32:3

1. Heavenly Father Speaks to Us through the Scriptures

Scripture

Search the scriptures; for in them ye think ye have eternal life: and they are they which testify of me.
—John 5:39

Visual Aid:

GAK 617

Illustration Ideas:

A telephone, the world, a set of scriptures, a heart, Heavenly Father

When Caleb's parents went away on a long trip, he had to stay with his grandma and grandpa. Caleb missed his parents while they were gone, but he loved to talk to them on the phone and tell them all about the things he was doing.

After we are born, we can't be with Heavenly Father face-to-face, but he still wants to talk to us, and one way he does is through the scriptures. Heavenly Father has always helped prophets record messages for us in the scriptures. When you read the scriptures, you will remember how much he loves you. You will want to choose the right so you can live with him again.

It's not enough to just read the scriptures every once in a while. You have to get in the habit of reading them every day so you can remember the lessons they teach. If you try hard, you will be able to find all the messages Heavenly Father has prepared for you in the scriptures.

Thought Question: How can you find the messages Heavenly Father is sending you in the scriptures?

2. I Can Enjoy Reading the Scriptures

In the Book of Mormon, Nephi told us that we are supposed to feast upon the words of Christ, which are the scriptures. But Nephi didn't mean that we should take big bites out of our scriptures. He was telling us to enjoy reading the scriptures in the same way we like to eat pizza or ice cream or whatever our favorite kinds of food are.

In the New Testament, Jesus told a parable about a king who sent out the invitations for a wonderful feast to his noble friends and family. But they told the king they were too busy or they didn't want to come. So instead, the king invited the common people in the towns around him.

Heavenly Father is like the king. He has invited you to come to his feast, but it's up to you to decide if you want to go. One way to accept his invitation is to continue studying the scriptures. As you do, they will become easier to understand, and you will grow to love them.

Thought Question: Why do you think we're supposed to "feast" on the words in the scriptures instead of just snacking on them or munching on them?

Scripture

Then saith he to his servants, The wedding is ready, but they which were bidden were not worthy. Go ye therefore into the highways, and as many as ye shall find, bid to the marriage.
—Matthew 22:8–9

Visual Aid:

GAB 65

Illustration Ideas:

Scriptures, your favorite food, Jesus, a castle, a feast, an invitation

3. I Can Find Answers in the Scriptures

Scripture

For I did liken all scriptures unto us, that it might be for our profit and learning.
—1 Nephi 19:23

Visual Aid:

GAK 302

Illustration Ideas:

A fortune cookie, a question mark, the Brass Plates, the Liahona, a treasure map

Have you ever cracked open a fortune cookie to find out your fortune? It's fun to do, but the best way to learn what you should do or what will happen to you is by reading the scriptures. Heavenly Father has given us the scriptures to teach us all the things we need to do to return to him. The scriptures can also give us answers to questions we're worrying about.

For example, when Nephi and Lehi didn't know which way to go in the wilderness, they used the brass plates to help them find answers. Heavenly Father gave them the Liahona to lead them in the right direction, but it would only work when they were reading their scriptures and choosing the right.

Heavenly Father loves you, and he has given you the scriptures to guide you. Just like a treasure map, the scriptures will lead you straight back to Heavenly Father if you continue to study them each day.

Thought Question: What could happen if you don't follow the directions you find in the scriptures?

4. I Can Have a Testimony of the Scriptures

In ancient Israel there lived a boy named Samuel. When Samuel was still young, his mother took him to live with the priests so he could spend his life serving Heavenly Father. Samuel learned many things from the priests about how to be righteous. One night, while Samuel was asleep, he heard a voice calling to him. Samuel thought it was Eli, one of the priests, so he ran to Eli's bed and said, "Here I am."

But Eli said, "I didn't call you. Just go back to bed."

After this happened three times, Eli finally realized what was going on. He told Samuel that the next time he heard the voice, he should answer it because the voice was really coming from the Lord. Samuel did what Eli said and learned many things from the Lord.

Sometimes it's hard to figure out how to listen to the Lord, but once you learn how, you can gain your very own testimony of the scriptures and the messages they contain.

Thought Question: What should you do if you don't understand a message that Heavenly Father gives you in the scriptures?

Scripture

And the Lord came, and stood, and called as at other times, Samuel, Samuel. Then Samuel answered, Speak; for thy servant heareth.
—*1 Samuel 3:10*

Visual Aid:

GAB 18

Illustration Ideas:

A boy, a bed, Jesus, the scriptures

Chapter 2

I Can Learn about Heavenly Father's Plan in the Scriptures

—Moses 1:39

1. Heavenly Father's Plan Will Help Me Return to Him.

Scripture

Verily I say unto you, Whatsoever ye shall bind on earth shall be bound in heaven: and whatsoever ye shall loose on earth shall be loosed in heaven.
—*Matthew 18:18*

Visual Aid:

GAB 119

Illustration Ideas:

A family, the temple, a baby, a child, an adult, heaven, Heavenly Father

Carmen and her family had been waiting for this day for almost two years—ever since they first met the missionaries. After their whole family was baptized, they began planning their trip to the temple to be sealed together. Carmen and her sister got to pick special dresses to wear in the temple, and everyone helped save enough money to pay for the trip. As Carmen walked into the temple, holding her mom's hand, she felt so happy to know that she was about to become part of a family that could be together forever.

Before we were born, Heavenly Father told us about a wonderful plan that would let us become just like him. We came to earth so we could follow that plan and join eternal families. No one is left out of Heavenly Father's family—as long as you choose the right, you will be part of a family that is together forever.

Thought Question: How can you prepare now to follow Heavenly Father's plan for the rest of your life?

8

2. Jesus Made a Special Place for Me

A long, long time ago, we all lived in heaven with Jesus and Heavenly Father. But we had learned everything we could in heaven and needed to go somewhere else to learn more. So, following Heavenly Father's instructions, Jesus created a place where we could have bodies and be separated from Heavenly Father for a little while. Jesus worked hard to make us this beautiful world. He created the water and the land, the light and the darkness, and all the plants and animals all around us. He even created the very first man and woman, named Adam and Eve.

Jesus and Heavenly Father love it when we thank them for the things they have given us. When we are grateful for their creations, it helps us to remember how much they love us and that we need to follow their plan so we can return to live with them someday.

Thought Question: How can you take good care of the earth that Jesus made for you?

Scripture

For the earth is full, and there is enough and to spare; yea, I prepared all things, and have given unto the children of men to be agents unto themselves.
—D&C 104:17

Visual Aid:

GAK 600

Illustration Ideas:

The earth, the sun, the moon, plants, animals, Adam and Eve, Jesus

3. My Family Is the Most Important Part of Heavenly Father's Plan

Scripture

And as I partook of the fruit thereof it filled my soul with exceedingly great joy; wherefore, I began to be desirous that my family should partake of it also; for I knew that it was desirable above all other fruit.
—1 Nephi 8:12

Visual Aid:

GAB 69

Illustration Ideas:

The iron rod, the tree of life, Laman and Lemuel, a family

Do you remember Lehi's dream in the Book of Mormon? When Lehi reached the beautiful tree, he found out that the fruit was sweet and special. He wanted to share it with his whole family, but in his dream only some of his family came to the tree and ate the fruit. This made Lehi sad.

Lehi knew that families are the most important part of Heavenly Father's plan. Two of Lehi's sons liked to grumble and complain and cause trouble. Lehi always worried about them because they kept making bad choices, but he never gave up on them. He wanted his whole family to make it back to Heavenly Father instead of only some of them, like in his dream.

Being in a family teaches us how to love and serve one another. Families bind us together and keep us safe from Satan. We all need to work hard to make sure our families hold on to the iron rod, so we can all make it back to Heavenly Father.

Thought Question: What would happen to the gospel if we didn't have families?

4. God Can Make Me Better if I Follow His Plan

When the pioneers left Nauvoo, many of them didn't know for sure where they were going. They had to rely on Heavenly Father and have faith that he would help them reach their destination. They knew that Heavenly Father was guiding them through their prophet, Brigham Young, and that Heavenly Father's plan for them was better than anything they could come up with on their own.

They walked and walked and walked for hundreds of miles and faced many scary things on their way. Some of them even died. But they all knew that what they were doing was right. They trusted Heavenly Father and Brigham Young, and eventually they made it to the Salt Lake Valley. There they built a city and lived in peace.

If we are righteous, we can make it back to Heavenly Father, just like the pioneers made it to Zion. Following Heavenly Father's plan helps us to become better than we ever could be on our own.

Thought Question: Will Heavenly Father ever force you to follow his plan?

Scripture

Trust in the Lord with all thine heart; and lean not unto thine own understanding. In all thy ways acknowledge him, and he shall direct thy paths.
—Proverbs 3:5–6

Visual Aid:

GAK 411

Illustration Ideas:

The pioneers, a covered wagon, a map, a compass, Brigham Young

Chapter 3

The Prophets Tell Me about Heavenly Father

—Doctrine and Covenants 1:38

1. Heavenly Father Leads Us through Prophets

Scripture

He that receiveth a prophet in the name of a prophet shall receive a prophet's reward.
—Matthew 10:41

Visual Aid:

GAB 137

Illustration Ideas:

Children playing "Follow the Leader," a prophet speaking at conference, the prophet working in his office, the world

One day, Jonah and his friends played "Follow the Leader." Jonah really wanted to be the leader because the leader got to show everyone else what to do. Finally, it was Jonah's turn. He hopped on one foot and spun in a circle, and everyone else did too. When he was too tired of spinning, he sat down on the floor. Everyone else followed him. Jonah decided it was fun to be the leader, but sometimes it was hard work too, especially if you got dizzy.

In our church, we have a very important leader called a prophet. The prophet makes sure the members of the Church do what God wants them to do by telling them what God reveals to him. The prophet loves everyone, and he works hard to be a good example for us. Even when he gets tired, he keeps doing Heavenly Father's work.

We can help our prophet by praying for him and by being obedient. When we follow the prophet, he will lead us back to Heavenly Father.

Thought Question: What are some things the prophet told us to do last time he spoke in general conference?

2. I Can Listen to the Prophet

Moses was chosen to take God's people, the Israelites, from Egypt to the promised land. But the Egyptians didn't want the Israelites to leave because they liked making the Israelites work hard in their homes and cities.

Moses knew that Pharaoh, the Egyptian leader, wouldn't want to let the Israelites go, but Moses also knew that God would help him. Moses met with Pharaoh and told him that God wanted the Israelites to leave Egypt. If Pharaoh wouldn't let them go, Moses warned him that God would send sickness and frogs and bugs and lots of other bad things. God did as Moses said he would until Pharaoh finally gave in and listened to the prophet.

We also need to listen to the prophet today. When we do what the prophet tells us to, we are safe from bad things. Following the prophet brings us great blessings and makes us feel happy and loved. We can show Heavenly Father that we love him by following his prophet.

Thought Question: "How can following the prophet help you to be happy?"

Scripture

And the Lord spake unto Moses, Go unto Pharaoh, and say unto him, Thus saith the Lord, Let my people go, that they may serve me.
—Exodus 8:1

Visual Aid:

GAB 14

Illustration Ideas:

Moses, a pyramid, Pharaoh, sick people, frogs, bugs, the Israelites following Moses away from Egypt

3. The Prophet Leads Our Church

Scripture

At length I came to the con-clusion that I must either remain in darkness and con-fusion, or else I must do as James directs, that is, ask of God. I at length came to the determination to "ask of God."
—*Joseph Smith—History 1:13*

Visual Aid:

GAK 403

Illustration Ideas:

Different church buildings, A grove of trees, Heavenly Father and Jesus Christ, Joseph Smith preaching

When Joseph Smith was a young boy, many people were confused about what God wanted them to do. Joseph couldn't figure out which church to join because none of them seemed right. He wished that he had someone who could tell him what to do.

One day, Joseph was studying the Bible and decided to pray. He went into the woods near his home and knelt down to ask for an answer. Heavenly Father and Jesus Christ appeared to Joseph and told him that none of the churches were correct because there were no prophets to speak with God and lead the people. Joseph learned that soon he would become a prophet.

Ever since Joseph Smith's time, a prophet has led the Church. Because the prophet talks to Heavenly Father all the time, the prophet knows what we should do. He guides us so we can choose the right. That's why it's so important to listen to the prophet and obey his teachings.

Thought Question: What would happen to the Church if we didn't have a prophet?

4. Following the Prophet Keeps Me Safe

Tori's dad gave the family a few rules before their big hike. Everyone had to stick together and no one could leave the path. It was hard for Tori to wait for everyone. She liked to run ahead to see what was coming up next. One time, she ran so far ahead that she couldn't see her parents any more. When she turned around, she realized she couldn't even see the path. Tori was lost. Lucky for Tori, her family soon found her. Getting lost was a little scary, so Tori made sure to follow her dad's rules for the rest of the hike so she could be safe and stay with her family.

The prophet gives us rules and directions so that we can stay safe with our families forever. There are many exciting things in the world around us, and it's easy to get lost and forget how to make it back to Heavenly Father. But if we listen to the prophet's warnings and obey his rules, we can be safe from Satan's power.

Thought Question: What can you do if you get lost from the path that the prophets have told you to stay on?

Scripture

For his word ye shall receive, as if from mine own mouth, in all patience and faith.
—D&C 21:5

Visual Aid:

GAB 137

Illustration Ideas:

Hiking boots, a trail, the prophet, a family listening to general conference together

Chapter 4

Jesus Suffered and Died for Me

—Articles of Faith 1:3

1. Jesus Loved Me Enough to Save Me

Scripture

Greater love hath no man than this, that a man lay down his life for his friends.
—John 15:13

Visual Aid:

GAK 608

Illustration Ideas:

Jesus, the earth, the cross, Jesus' empty tomb

Think about all the people who love you: your parents, your primary teachers, your brothers and sisters, and your friends. But Jesus loves us so much that he died to save us.

Before we came to earth, Heavenly Father knew that none of us would be able to stay perfect for our whole lives. We would need someone to save us so we could come back and live with him instead of having to suffer for our sins forever.

Both Jesus and Satan offered to help us return to Heavenly Father, but Satan didn't care about us. He just wanted everyone to worship him. Jesus knew that Heavenly Father's plan was best. He offered to die for us, even though he knew it would be very hard and painful. Everyone who agreed to follow Heavenly Father's plan was allowed to come to earth and get a body. We chose to follow Jesus before we were born because we knew he loved us and would look out for us.

Thought Question: How can you show Jesus that you still love and trust him like you did before you were born?

2. I Can Be Perfect if I Follow Jesus' Example

Sabrina has a younger sister named Kylie. Everything that Sabrina does, Kylie wants to do too. When Sabrina draws a picture or plays soccer, Kylie wants to do those things too. Sabrina doesn't like to eat carrots, so Kylie doesn't eat them either. Their mom tells Sabrina that it's important to try and set a good example for Kylie.

Each of us has an older brother who we can always follow. His name is Jesus, and he is the perfect example for us. He never sinned or made a mistake, so we should try not to sin too. He was baptized, so we should be baptized too. And he loved everyone, especially little children. That's how we know that we need to love one another.

When we choose to follow a different example instead of Jesus, we might have fun for a little while, but we will never be really happy. But if we repent and follow the example Jesus set, we will become perfect someday, and then we will be able to live with Heavenly Father again.

Thought Question: Is there any other way to become perfect except by following Jesus' example?

Scripture

Come unto me, all ye that labour and are heavy laden, and I will give you rest. Take my yoke upon you, and learn of me; for I am meek and lowly in heart: and ye shall find rest unto your souls.
—Matthew 11:28–29

Visual Aid:

GAB 1

Illustration Ideas:

Crayons, a soccer ball, carrots, someone being baptized, Jesus Christ

3. The Atonement Lets Me Return to Heavenly Father

Scripture

While I was harrowed up by the memory of my many sins . . . I remembered also to have heard my father prophesy unto the people concerning the coming of one Jesus Christ, a Son of God, to atone for the sins of the world.
—*Alma 36:17*

Visual Aid:

GAB 77
GAK 227

Illustration Ideas:

Alma the Younger, an angel, an olive tree, happy faces, sad faces

When he was a teenager, Alma the Younger didn't keep the commandments, and he even tried to destroy the church. Then an angel came and told him to stop being disobedient. At first, Alma didn't think he could change. He thought that he would feel sad about the bad things he had done forever.

Because of the Atonement, we don't have to suffer forever. Instead, we can repent and find forgiveness. It is impossible for us to understand just how hard the Atonement was for Jesus to perform. Even though it is sad that Jesus suffered, thinking about the Atonement should make us happy because it reminds us of how much how much Jesus loves us.

Alma the Younger remembered that Heavenly Father and Jesus love him. He knew that through the Atonement, he could repent and be forgiven. It was hard to do, but Alma the Younger started choosing the right and eventually became a great prophet.

Thought Question: How can Jesus understand how it feels to sin, even though he was perfect?

4. I Will Live Again after I Die

Uncle Max was so fun to be around, and Charlie loved it when Uncle Max scooped him up and carried him on his shoulders. When Uncle Max died, Charlie went to the funeral with his parents, but it didn't seem like Uncle Max was really gone. Charlie's mom explained what had happened to Uncle Max after he died. She said even though Uncle Max's body had stopped working, his spirit was still alive. Someday, Uncle Max would be resurrected and his body and spirit would be back together again. Charlie was happy to know that someday Uncle Max would be able to do all the things he could do with his body.

After we die, each of us will be resurrected. When Jesus was resurrected after he died on the cross, he made it possible for all of us to live again. Someday, after Jesus returns to earth, all of us will have glorious new bodies that won't get sick or hurt. This will be a wondrous event for all of us.

Thought Question: How can you show Jesus how thankful you are for the gift of being resurrected someday?

Scripture

For God so loved the world, that he gave his only begotten Son, that whosoever believeth in him should not perish, but have everlasting life.
—*John 3:16*

Visual Aid:

GAK 245

Illustration Ideas:

A coffin, a boy at a cemetery, a spirit body, the same boy looking happy

Chapter 5

Jesus' Church Is on the Earth Again

—Joseph Smith—History 1:17

1. This is the Same Church that Jesus Created

Scripture

We believe in the same organization that existed in the primitive church. Namely, apostles, prophets, pastors, teachers, evangelists and so forth.
—Articles of Faith 1:6

Visual Aid:

GAB 38

Illustration Ideas:

Jesus giving the priesthood to his apostles, Joseph Smith receiving the priesthood from Peter, James, and John

When Jesus was on the earth, he knew that he would only have a short time to be with his disciples, so he wanted to be sure they could continue his church after he died. He organized a quorum of twelve apostles and gave them the priesthood, which is the name for God's power and authority that Jesus used while he was on the earth. But only a few years after his death, almost all of his apostles were killed too. Jesus' church started changing, and pretty soon, they no longer had the priesthood.

Nearly two thousand years later, Joseph Smith received a marvelous vision. Heavenly Father and Jesus told him they would help him restore the same church that Jesus had in his time, with the same organization, teachings, and authority.

Now that the gospel has been fully restored, we can enjoy all the blessings Heavenly Father has prepared for us. We can be happy when we think of all the great things Heavenly Father has given us in our church.

Thought Question: Why did Joseph Smith need to restore Jesus' church instead of making a brand new one?

2. Joseph Smith Restored Jesus' Church

Devin is the best batter on his baseball team. But sometimes Devin's games are on Sundays. He doesn't really mind not playing, but his teammates always make fun of him or tell him to play anyway. When this happens, Devin remembers the example of Joseph Smith.

Joseph experienced the First Vision as a young man. This was the beginning of the Restoration, but at first, not many people believed Joseph. In fact, a lot of his friends and neighbors made fun of him or told him he was crazy. Joseph learned to ignore their teasing and focus on restoring the gospel. He knew it didn't matter what anyone else said as long as he obeyed Heavenly Father.

We can follow Joseph's example by doing the right thing, no matter what. When we feel discouraged, we can remember Joseph Smith. Joseph received many great blessings as part of the Restoration, and Heavenly Father will bless us also as we try to obey him.

Thought Question: What teachings did Joseph Smith restore that affect me and my family today?

Scripture

And while they were persecuting me, reviling me . . . I was led to say in my heart: Why persecute me for telling the truth?
—Joseph Smith—History 1:25

Visual Aid:

GAB 97

Illustration Ideas:

A baseball bat, Joseph Smith, the Book of Mormon, a temple, a family

3. I Can Learn More about Jesus in the Book of Mormon

Scripture

We believe the Bible to be the word of God as far as it is translated correctly; we also believe the Book of Mormon to be the word of God.
—Articles of Faith 1:8

Visual Aid:

GAK 326

Illustration Ideas:

Two girls, a Bible, a Book of Mormon, Nephites, Joseph Smith, the Golden Plates

Hannah and Chelsea are best friends, even though they don't go to the same church. Chelsea believes in Jesus, but she doesn't believe that Joseph Smith was a prophet or that the Book of Mormon is true like Hannah does.

What Chelsea doesn't understand is that the Book of Mormon talks about many of the things she already believes in. In the Book of Mormon, we learn about Christ and his Atonement, just like we do in the Bible. But the Book of Mormon also contains more truth. It teaches us about the plan that Jesus and Heavenly Father created for us to return to them someday. From the Book of Mormon, we also learn how much Heavenly Father loves all his children, no matter where they live or what they look like. The Book of Mormon is one of the most precious gifts of the Restoration. When we read it, we experience great power.

Thought Question: What parts of the gospel would be confusing if we only had the Bible?

4. Jesus' Power Is Back on the Earth

Jairus was a powerful man, but he didn't have enough power to keep his daughter from getting sick. When his daughter was about to die, he had to rely on another power. He had heard that Jesus could perform miracles, so he hurried to find Jesus.

When Jairus told Jesus about his daughter, Jesus agreed to heal her. But on the way back, one of Jairus's servants told him his daughter had died. Jesus told everyone not to worry because the girl was only sleeping. Finally, Jesus and Jairus arrived at the house. Jesus told the girl to get up from her bed, and she did. Jairus knew the miracle was only possible because Jesus had the power of God.

Today, we have this same power. It is called the priesthood. After Jesus' apostles died, the priesthood was lost for many years, but then Peter, James, and John appeared to Joseph Smith and Oliver Cowdery to restore the priesthood. We are so blessed to have the power of God in our church.

Thought Question: How has the priesthood helped you?

Scripture

And behold, there cometh one of the rulers of the synagogue . . . saying, My little daughter lieth at the point of death: I pray thee, come and lay thy hands on her, that she may be healed; and she shall live.
—Mark 5:22–23

Visual Aid:

GAB 41

Illustration Ideas:

Jesus, Jairus, the apostles, Joseph Smith and Oliver Cowdery receiving the priesthood

Chapter 6

Faith, Repentance, Baptism, and the Holy Ghost Help Me to Follow God's Plan

—Articles of Faith 1:4

1. I Can Learn and Grow When I Have Faith in Jesus

Scripture

And after the brother of Jared had beheld the finger of the Lord . . . the Lord could not withhold anything from his sight; wherefore he showed him all things, for he could no longer be kept without the veil.
—Ether 12:21

Visual Aid:

GAK 318

Illustration Ideas:

Jaredite barges, clear stones, Jesus' finger, Jesus with the brother of Jared

The brother of Jared had a problem. He had built boats so his people could get to the promised land, but he didn't know how to put light in the boats. He was worried, but he also had faith that Jesus would help him. He gathered sixteen small stones and asked the Lord to touch them with his finger so they would glow. Jesus was so pleased with the brother of Jared's faith that he showed himself to the brother of Jared.

Faith allows us to do great things because even if we can't do something alone, Heavenly Father can do anything. When we have faith in Jesus, we know that he will help us, no matter what our problems are. Having faith helps us love Jesus and feel his love for us. Our faith will make sure that we can do everything Heavenly Father needs us to do, no matter what.

Thought Question: What things have you been able to do because of your faith?

2. When I Repent, I Can Be Forgiven

Saul did not believe in Jesus until one day when Jesus appeared to him and told Saul to stop hurting the people of his church. From that day on, Saul became a believer. It must have taken a lot of courage for Saul to face the people he hurt and ask them to forgive him, but he did it. Saul believed that if he would repent, he could be forgiven. He was so determined to change that he even changed his name from Saul to Paul.

When you make a wrong choice, you need to change too. You can do this by using the Atonement. Even if you make mistakes, Heavenly Father always loves you and wants you to repent. When you repent and take the sacrament, you accept Jesus' Atonement, which means you don't have to suffer like he did. Heavenly Father is so happy when you repent. He loves to forgive you because he knows that if you keep trying, one day you will be able to live with him again.

Thought Question: What would happen if you didn't repent after you did something wrong?

Scripture

All that heard him were amazed. . . . But Saul increased the more in strength, and confounded the Jews which dwelt at Damascus, proving that this is very Christ.
—Acts 9:21–22

Visual Aid:

GAB 61

Illustration Ideas:

Saul, Jesus, Saul preaching, the sacrament

3. Baptism Is a Covenant

Scripture

If this be the desire of your hearts, what have you against being baptized in the name of the Lord, as a witness before him that ye have entered into a covenant with him, that ye will serve him and keep his commandments, that he may pour out his Spirit more abundantly upon you?
—Mosiah 18:10

Visual Aid:

GAB 104

Illustration Ideas:

A boy, a baptismal font, white clothes, a church building, the sacrament

Jack couldn't wait to be baptized because he knew how important it was. During the baptism meeting, Jack tried to pay attention, but he was so excited it was hard to listen. When Jack entered the font, he had a big smile on his face, and as he came out of the water, he felt so clean and warm. He knew Heavenly Father was happy with him.

It is so important to be baptized because baptism is the first covenant we make with Heavenly Father. A covenant is a sacred two-way promise that helps us remember how much Heavenly Father loves us. At baptism, we promise to always remember Heavenly Father and follow his commandments. Heavenly Father promises to bless us for doing the right things.

When we take the sacrament each week, we should remember how Jesus suffered and what it means to be baptized. Taking the sacrament reverently can make us clean and whole again, just like baptism.

Thought Question: Why do you have to be eight years old in order to be baptized?

4. The Holy Ghost Can Always Be with Me

Before Ammon and his brothers came to teach them, the Lamanites didn't know about Heavenly Father. The king of all the Lamanites heard about God from Aaron, one of Ammon's brothers. Even though he hadn't been baptized, the king felt the Spirit. Then he prayed to know if God was real. He said that he would give away all his sins to know God and have God's spirit with him.

This Lamanite king showed great faith. When he prayed, he relied on the Holy Ghost to help him know the truth. Because he doesn't have a body, the Holy Ghost can be with us all the time. He can be a special friend who helps you be happy when you're sad and tells you the right things to do. The gift of the Holy Ghost is one thing that makes being a member of The Church of Jesus Christ of Latter-day Saints so special.

Thought Question: How can you make sure that the Holy Ghost can be with you when you need him?

Scripture

O God, Aaron hath told me that there is a God; and if there is a God, and if thou art God, wilt thou make thyself known unto me, and I will give away all my sins to know thee.
—*Alma 22:18*

Visual Aid:

GAK 602

Illustration Ideas:

Aaron, King Lamoni's Father, the Holy Ghost with Heavenly Father and Jesus, a child praying

Chapter 7

I Can Be with God in the Temple.

—The Family: A Proclamation to the World,
paragraph 3

1. God Has Always Visited His People in the Temple

Scripture

And I, Nephi, did build a temple; and I did construct it after the manner of the temple of Solomon. . . . And the workmanship thereof was exceedingly fine.
—2 Nephi 5:16

Visual Aid:

GAB 52

Illustration Ideas:

A modern temple, Solomon's temple, Nephi, a family

One of the best things about being alive today is that if you are righteous, you will be able to enter the temple someday to be closer to Heavenly Father.

In ancient times, only a few people got to go inside the temple. The Israelites constructed a few temples and the Nephites also had some temples, but it wasn't until Joseph Smith restored the gospel that we could do temple work like we do today.

Throughout time, temples have been sacred, special places for Heavenly Father's children to be with him. A temple is a house of God. This means that when God comes to the earth, he can come to the temple. Inside the temple, everything is quiet, clean, and still. It is a place to stop worrying about other things and focus all your attention on Heavenly Father. We are blessed to have so many temples where we can be with God.

Thought Question: When was the last time you visited a temple?

2. My Family Can Be Together Forever

Adam and Eve were the first people on the earth and that meant they were the first parents. They had to teach their children about Heavenly Father's plan. Some of their children were good and righteous. Others made bad choices. But Adam and Eve loved their children and wanted to be with them all forever.

Everyone has a family just like Adam and Eve did. Being part of a family doesn't mean that you always get along with your family members. The important thing is to keep trying to make good choices so you can be with them forever.

The covenants you will make in the temple will link you to your family both here on earth and in heaven after you die. Being part of an eternal family is so important because families are the best part of Heavenly Father's plan.

Thought Question: What could you do to help your family members love each other more?

Scripture
And Adam and Eve blessed the name of God, and they made all things known unto their sons and their daughters.
—*Moses 5:12*

Visual Aid:

GAB 5

Illustration Ideas:

Adam and Eve, children learning, the temple, a family

3. The Pioneers Built Temples so They Could Be with God

Scripture

Behold, this is the tithing and the sacrifice which I, the Lord, require at their hands, that there may be a house built unto me for the salvation of Zion.
—D&C 97:12

Visual Aid:

GAK 502

Illustration Ideas:

Pioneers, Brigham Young, big blocks of granite, a half-built temple, people praying, the Salt Lake Temple

When Brigham Young led the pioneers into the Salt Lake Valley, one of the first things he did was show them where they would build the temple. The people were tired after their long trek. Some probably thought it would be more important to build houses than a temple. But Brigham Young knew that God needed a house too.

Satan doesn't like it when we build temples because he knows how important they are to Heavenly Father's plan. It took the pioneers forty years to finish the Salt Lake Temple because of all the ways Satan tried to stop them. They had to just keep working. Many people gave up their most precious things to build the temple.

When we visit the temple, we can remember how much the early saints sacrificed. Being part of the Church still means we have to make sacrifices and work hard. Heavenly Father's kingdom is still growing, and we can help it spread throughout the world.

Thought Question: What kinds of sacrifices do you have to make as a member of the Church?

4. Someday I Will Go to the Temple

Jesus told a story about ten girls who were going to a wedding. The girls had to wait a long time and keep their lamps lit with oil until the bridegroom came to take them to the wedding. Five of them were wise and brought extra oil. The other five were foolish and didn't have enough. While they went to get more, the bridegroom came. The foolish girls didn't get to go to the wedding.

Just like the wise girls, we need to be prepared so we can be ready when Heavenly Father asks us to do something. One thing he wants us all to do is go to the temple. It might seem like going to the temple is something that will happen a long time from now. But you have to start preparing now so you'll be ready when the time comes.

Heavenly Father is excited to see you in his house. If you prepare now, someday, when you enter the temple, you will know that you are clean and worthy to be there.

Thought Question: What could you do today to help you be ready to enter the temple?

Scripture

Watch therefore, for ye know neither the day nor the hour wherein the Son of man cometh.
—*Matthew 25:13*

Visual Aid:

GAB 53

Illustration Ideas:

A girl, oil, a lamp, a groom, a bride, the temple, Heavenly Father

Chapter 8

Heavenly Father Gave Me a Body Just Like His

—1 Corinthians 3:16–17

1. Heavenly Father Gave Me a Body

Scripture

Now, this restoration shall come to all . . . and even there shall not so much as a hair of their heads be lost; but every thing shall be restored to its perfect frame.
—Alma 11:44

Visual Aid:

GAB 59

Illustration Ideas:

A wheelchair, something to eat, something to smell, something to touch, something to hear, a girl jumping

Isabel has never been able to walk. She was born with a disease that kept her body from growing the right way, so she uses a wheelchair to get around. Sometimes Isabel wishes she could walk and run like her friends, but her parents remind her that her body is a great gift.

Each of us has also been given a body. We use our bodies to do lots of things. We use them to see, hear, speak, smell, and touch. We can also use them to do good things for other people.

Everyone has a different body, but all of us can honor our bodies by keeping ourselves clean and healthy. Someday, we will all be resurrected and given perfect bodies. When this happens to Isabel, her body won't be sick anymore, so she will be able to walk and do all the things her friends do. No matter what your body looks like, you can do good things with it and show Heavenly Father how much you love the body he gave you.

Thought Question: What do you like about your body?

2. I Can Honor My Body by Dressing Modestly

What do a policeman, a chef, and a scientist all have in common? Each of them wear special clothes when they go to work. Their clothes help them do their jobs. A policeman wears his uniform so people know who to ask for help if something bad happens. A chef wears clean clothes and a big hat to keep his kitchen clean. And a scientist wears a coat to protect himself from chemicals.

Even though you probably don't wear a uniform or go to work yet, your clothes still tell people who you are and what you do. When you wear clean, modest clothes, people can see that you know how special your body is, and they will think you are special too. Wearing modest clothing shows everyone that you are working to build Heavenly Father's kingdom.

You can show Heavenly Father how much you love your body by dressing modestly. When you show respect for your body, you also show respect for Heavenly Father.

Thought Question: What could you do to show others that you enjoy being modest?

Scripture

And again, thou shalt not be proud in thy heart; let all thy garments be plain, and their beauty the beauty of the work of thine own hands.
—D&C 42:40

Visual Aid:

GAB 120

Illustration Ideas:

A policeman, a chef, a scientist, modest clothes for a girl, modest clothes for a boy

3. I Can Honor My Body by Obeying the Word of Wisdom

Scripture

And at the end of ten days their countenances appeared fairer and fatter in flesh than all the children which did eat the portion of the king's meat.
—Daniel 1:15

Visual Aid:

GAK 603
GAB 23

Illustration Ideas:

A Babylonian palace, a plate of meat, coffee, tea, a cigarette, fruits and vegetables, bread, meat, a TV, junk food

Daniel was a young Israelite who went to live in a Babylonian palace. When he arrived, he asked if he could have different food, since the food they were serving in the palace was against the rules God had given him. The Babylonians didn't understand why Daniel wouldn't eat their food, but he convinced them to let him try it. After just ten days, Daniel looked healthier and happier than anyone else. Heavenly Father blessed him for being obedient.

Heavenly Father expects us to treat our bodies well by eating the right things. That way we will have the energy to do the things he needs us to do. He has also told us that we need to be active and not spend too much time sleeping or just watching TV and eating junk food.

Together, all of these rules make up the Word of Wisdom. By following the Word of Wisdom, we show Heavenly Father that we can take good care of the bodies he has given us.

Thought Question: Do you have any bad habits you can change to better follow the Word of Wisdom?

4. I Want My Mind and Body to Be Clean

One time Aiden was playing football outside when it started to rain. Pretty soon the whole field was muddy. When the game was over, Aiden had mud on his hands, on his knees, and almost everywhere else. His parents took him home and helped him get clean again.

Just like we need to keep our bodies clean, we also need to keep our minds clean. But it can be hard to see the mud that gets into our minds. Some things that can make our minds muddy are bad music, movies, or books. Even a little mud can keep us from being clean. And when our minds aren't clean, we can't have the Spirit. Without the Spirit, it gets harder and harder to see the mud. Pretty soon we just feel icky and sad all the time.

When we repent, we can take away all the mud in our minds. Then the Spirit can guide us to good, happy things so we can keep our minds clean and not let any mud get in.

Thought Question: How could you encourage your friends to listen to and watch good things?

Scripture
If there is anything virtuous, lovely, or of good report or praiseworthy, we seek after these things.
—*Articles of Faith 1:13*

Visual Aid:
GAK 605

Illustration Ideas:
A football jersey, lots of mud, clean and folded clothes, a CD or an iPod, some movies, a stack of books, a computer

Chapter 9

Someday Everyone Will Hear the Gospel

—Doctrine and Covenants 133:37

1. The Gospel Is for Everyone

Scripture

Behold, the field is white already to harvest; therefore whoso desireth to reap, let him thrust in his sickle with his might, and reap while the day lasts, that he may treasure up for his soul everlasting salvation in the kingdom of God.
—D&C 6:3

Visual Aid:

GAK 612

Illustration Ideas:

Samuel Smith, a field of long grass, the world, two missionaries

Joseph Smith had a younger brother named Samuel. After Samuel learned about the gospel, he wanted to share it with others. Samuel was one of the very first missionaries during the Restoration. These early missionaries had to work hard and walk a long way to spread the gospel. Sometimes the people were kind to them, but other times they were mean and didn't want to hear anything about the Church.

In the Doctrine and Covenants, there are many revelations that talk about a white field that is ready to be harvested. This field represents the world and how it is full of people who are ready to hear the gospel. The scriptures say that the most important part of being a good missionary is being willing to work. If you work hard to be a good missionary, Heavenly Father will bless you with everything else you need. Sometimes it's hard to be a good missionary, but sharing the gospel can be a great blessing.

Thought Question: What could you do to help spread the gospel to the rest of the world?

2. Heavenly Father Blesses Everyone through Missionary Work

Ammon and his three brothers decided to do something dangerous. They would go to the land of the Lamanites and preach the gospel to their enemies. At first, it was hard, but later this became one of the best times in the history of the Book of Mormon, all because Ammon and his brothers decided to be missionaries.

Heavenly Father loves to bless us when we do good things, and missionaries do so many good things that they have leftover blessings to share with their families, their ward members, and the people they teach.

A missionary's letters to his family can bless them by keeping them connected to him and each other. Ward members are blessed with new friends when they invite the missionaries over for dinner or to teach a lesson. And the people who take the missionary discussions are blessed to feel the Spirit and join the Church. In the end, the whole world is blessed because of our missionaries.

Thought Question: What leftover blessings have you received from the missionaries in your ward?

Scripture

Go forth among the Lamanites . . . and establish my word; yet ye shall be patient in long-suffering and afflictions, that ye may show forth good examples unto them in me, and I will make an instrument of thee in my hands unto the salvation of many souls.
—Alma 17:11

Visual Aid:

GAB 115

Illustration Ideas:

Ammon and his brothers, King Mosiah, a letter, dinner, some missionaries doing service

3. Someday I Will Serve a Mission

Scripture

I perceive that thou art a sober child, and art quick to observe; Therefore . . . when ye are [twenty-four years old] go to the land Antum unto a hill which shall be called Shim; and there have I deposited unto the Lord all the sacred engravings concerning this people.
—Mormon 1:2–3

Visual Aid:

GAK 306

Illustration Ideas:

A young Nephite boy, a Nephite battleground, a missionary name badge, the scriptures, a piggy bank and some coins

When Mormon was only ten years old, a prophet told him about the records he would be in charge of one day. When he was sixteen, he began leading the Nephites in battle. And at twenty years old, Mormon defeated the Lamanite king.

Like Mormon, we all have special things we need to accomplish. For many people, that will include serving a full-time mission. Mormon's story teaches that it's never too early to begin preparing for your mission. One of the most important ways to prepare is by gaining your own testimony of the gospel. Another thing you can do right now is start saving a missionary fund. You can even be a missionary now by inviting your friends to come with you to church activities or meetings.

If you begin preparing early, you will be ready to serve whenever the Lord needs you, and that will be a great blessing for your whole life.

Thought Question: What can you do now to prepare for the things Heavenly Father wants you to do with your life?

4. Sharing the Gospel Makes Me Happy

Usually Liam was good at sharing, but one time Liam's sister Maggie tried to take his favorite toy sword while he was playing with it. Liam and Maggie both pulled hard, and suddenly the sword broke. Liam was so sad and angry. His mom held him while he cried, and then she reminded him how much better things would have gone if he had let Maggie have a turn. If Liam and Maggie had shared the sword, they would have both been happy and the sword wouldn't have broken.

One of the most important things we need to share is the gospel. The good thing about the gospel is that you don't have to let someone else have a turn with it because you can both have it at the same time. There are many things about the gospel that make us happy. And when we share the gospel with others, they can have those happy things too.

Thought Question: Can you think of a friend you could share the gospel with?

Scripture

And if it so be that you should labor all your days in crying repentance unto this people, and bring, save it be one soul unto me, how great shall be your joy with him in the kingdom of my Father!
—D&C 18:15

Visual Aid:

GAB 109 and 110

Illustration Ideas:

A toy sword, a broken sword, a Book of Mormon, a church building, two friends talking

Chapter 10

I Can Talk to Heavenly Father When I Pray

—James 1:5

1. Heavenly Father Wants Me to Talk to Him

Scripture

My beloved son, Moroni . . . I am mindful of you always in my prayers, continually praying unto God the Father in the name of his Holy Child, Jesus, that he, through his infinite goodness and grace, will keep you through the endurance of faith on his name to the end.
—Moroni 8:2–3

Visual Aid:

GAK 319

Illustration Ideas:

Mormon, Moroni, a letter, a child praying

The book of Moroni contains a few letters that Mormon sent to his son Moroni while they were fighting the Lamanites. These letters were full of guidance and direction. They told Moroni how much Mormon cared about him. After Mormon died, Moroni could read these letters to remember his father.

These days we don't write very many letters because we have other ways to communicate that are faster and easier. But there is one method of communication that was used by Mormon and Moroni and is still used by us today. It's prayer.

When you pray, you can tell Heavenly Father about everything that is happening in your life. And just like Mormon's letters helped Moroni to fight his battles, when Heavenly Father answers our prayers it helps us to keep trying and to follow his commandments.

Thought Question: How do you know when your prayers have been answered?

2. When I Read the Scriptures, I Can Learn to Pray the Right Way

Almost every kind of animal can make a sound. Ducks quack, cows moo, and mice squeak. Animals make noises to send messages to the other animals around them. Even animals know that talking can help make everyone happier and more safe. Animals don't have to learn how to make noise because they already know how when they're born. But when we are born, we don't know how to say words, and we especially don't know how to talk to Heavenly Father. That's why he gave us the scriptures.

Heavenly Father expects us to learn from the examples in the scriptures so that we can talk to him and he can talk to us. Heavenly Father loves it when we pray to him. When we pray the right way, we show Heavenly Father that we care more about what he wants than what we want. This is important because he always wants to help us be better than we could be on our own.

Thought Question: Why is it important to pray the way Heavenly Father wants you to pray?

Scripture
But thou, when thou prayest, enter into thy closet, and when thou hast shut thy door, pray to thy Father who is in secret; and thy Father, who seeth in secret, shall reward thee openly.
—3 Nephi 13:6

Visual Aid:
GAB 84

Illustration Ideas:
A duck, a cow, a mouse, the scriptures, Heavenly Father, a child praying

3. I Can Know that Heavenly Father Hears Me

Scripture

The scriptures are laid before thee, yea, and all things denote there is a God; yea, even the earth, and all things that are upon the face of it, yea, and its motion, yea, and also all the planets which move in their regular form do witness that there is a Supreme Creator.
—Alma 30:44

Visual Aid:

GAK 100

Illustration Ideas:

Thunderclouds, birds, the world, a child praying, Heavenly Father

In our church hymnbook, there is a song called "How Great Thou Art." It tells how the things all around us teach us about God. Jesus and Heavenly Father created this beautiful world to help us remember them. Like the song says, when we hear thunderclouds rumbling, we can remember how powerful God is. Or when we hear birds singing, we can remember how sweet and gentle God is.

But even with all of Heavenly Father's beautiful creations to remind them, there are many people in the world who don't believe God is real. This is because they don't know how to pray or they've never learned how to recognize the answers to their prayers.

Most of the time, our prayers are answered in small and simple ways, not with big visions or miracles. Sometimes the only answer we get is a warm, peaceful feeling that everything will be okay. God loves you. He is always waiting to answer your prayers.

Thought Question: What things remind you that Heavenly Father loves you?

4. I Can Know Heavenly Father Will Answer My Prayers

Alma said that we should pretend that the word of God is a seed. When you plant a seed in the ground, you have to take care of it for a long time before it grows into a plant. Even though it looks like nothing is happening, if you keep watering the seed and giving it just enough sunlight, the seed will sprout and grow into a strong and healthy tree.

When we first learn about prayer, it's like a seed that we plant in the ground. At first we have to water that seed by continuing to pray and choose the right. Our prayers will change from seeds to plants when we recognize how Heavenly Father is answering them. Sometimes it might look like nothing is happening when we pray. This is because Heavenly Father knows what is best for us better than we do.

No matter how or when our answers come, our job is to keep praying and have faith that our prayers will be answered.

Thought Question: What things help you to water your seed of faith?

Scripture

Behold if it be a . . .good seed . . . it will begin to swell within your breasts; and when you feel these swelling motions, ye will begin to say within yourselves—It must needs be that this is a good seed, or that the word is good, for it beginneth to enlarge my soul; yea, it beginneth to enlighten my understanding, yea, it beginneth to be delicious to me.
—Alma 32:28

Visual Aid:

GAK 100

Illustration Ideas:

A seed, a watering bucket, a little plant, a tree, a child praying

Chapter 11

Heavenly Father Knows I Love Him When I Am Reverent

—Matthew 22:37

1. I Can Show Heavenly Father I Love Him by Being Reverent

Scripture

Ye shall keep my sabbaths, and reverence my sanctuary: I am the Lord.
—Leviticus 19:30

Visual Aid:

GAK 610

Illustration Ideas:

A house, grandparents, a temple, a church building

Lyddie's grandparents live in a very nice house, filled with things they've collected from all over the world. Whenever Lyddie comes to visit, she loves to look at all the pretty things on her grandparent's bookshelves, but Lyddie knows that she needs to ask before touching any of them. If her grandparents say it's okay, she needs to be very careful with their things so she doesn't break or lose them. Lyddie loves her grandparents, so she wants to be extra careful with their precious things.

When we go to church, we need to show the same kind of respect for Heavenly Father's house that Lyddie shows at her grandparents' house. We love Heavenly Father, so we need to treat his house and the things in it with reverence. When we are reverent in Heavenly Father's house, we show him how grateful we are for all of the blessings he has given us.

Thought Question: How could you show more reverence while you're at church?

2. The Sacrament Is an Important Time to Be Reverent

When Jesus visited the Nephites in America, one of the most important things he did was teach them how to administer the sacrament. He told the Nephites that the bread was a symbol of his body, which he sacrificed for each of us. The water was a symbol of his blood, which he shed for us.

Whenever you take the sacrament, you should remember how much Jesus suffered for you. Remembering Jesus can remind you that you don't have to suffer if you repent. Since the sacrament is so important, you need to be extra reverent while it is happening. Try to be as still and quiet as you can so that everyone in the meeting can feel the Spirit.

When you are reverent during the sacrament, you set a good example for those around you and you help them remember how much Jesus loves them.

Thought Question: What things usually distract you during the sacrament?

Scripture

And this shall ye do in remembrance of my body, which I have shown unto you. And it shall be a testimony unto the Father that ye do always remember me. And if ye do always remember me ye shall have my Spirit to be with you.
—3 Nephi 18:7

Visual Aid:

GAK 318

Illustration Ideas:

Jesus, Nephites, bread, water, children folding their arms

3. When I Am Reverent, I Can Feel the Spirit of God

Scripture

And when the Lord saw that he turned aside to see, God called unto him out of the midst of the bush, and said, Moses, Moses. And he said, Here am I. And he said, Draw not nigh hither: put off thy shoes from off thy feet, for the place whereon thou standest is holy ground.
—*Exodus 3:4–5*

Visual Aid:

GAB 13

Illustration Ideas:

Moses, the burning bush, shoes or sandals, a child jumping, a child being reverent

Heavenly Father needed Moses to perform a special mission, so one day, the Lord appeared to him in a flame. The flame was inside a bush, but the bush wasn't burning. Moses thought this was strange, so he decided to get a closer look. As he walked toward the bush, he heard the Lord speaking to him. Jesus told Moses to take off his shoes because he was standing on holy ground.

Today, God doesn't need to appear to us in burning bushes because we already have many sacred places for him to come and speak with us. These places are our temples and church buildings. When we visit a sacred place, we don't have to take off our shoes, but we do need to remember to show reverence so that the Spirit can be there with us. Showing respect for sacred places is so important because it brings us peace and helps us to remember what it is like to be with Heavenly Father.

Thought Question: How can you know when you are in a holy place?

4. Being Reverent Makes Me a Better Friend

Marco loves Church because he gets to see all his friends. Sometimes he and his friends are so excited to see each other that they start talking in loud voices. Then their teacher has to remind them to be quiet and listen. Marco tries very hard to be reverent. When his friends want to talk to him, he tells them he'll talk later. He wants to be a good friend and listen to what they have to say, but he knows that being a good friend means being a friend to Heavenly Father first.

Just like Marco, you can be a good friend to Heavenly Father when you listen in Primary and try to remember what your teacher says. Being reverent in church shows Heavenly Father you care about him. And when you care about Heavenly Father, you automatically have more love to give to other people, like your friends. Being reverent makes you a better friend, a better family member, and a better follower of Jesus Christ.

Thought Question: How could you remind yourself to be reverent at church, even when your friends want to play?

Scripture

And when thy people transgress, any of them, they may speedily repent and return unto thee, and find favor in thy sight, and be restored to the blessings which thou hast ordained to be poured out upon those who shall reverence thee in thy house.
—D&C 109:21

Visual Aid:

GAK 607

Illustration Ideas:

A group of friends talking and laughing, a church building, a child praying, ears (to listen quietly), a happy face

Chapter 12

I Can Learn about Jesus' Birth and Second Coming from the Scriptures

—Matthew 16:27

1. Jesus' Birth Was Foretold

Scripture

For unto us a child is born, unto us a son is given: and the government shall be upon his shoulder: and his name shall be called Wonderful, Counsellor, The mighty God, The everlasting Father, the Prince of Peace.
—Isaiah 9:6

Visual Aid:

GAK 113

Illustration Ideas:

Isaiah, the scriptures, baby Jesus, Jesus at the Second Coming

Isaiah lived a long time before Jesus was born, and he wrote some of the most important scriptures we have today. Because of his faith, Isaiah was able to learn about Jesus' teachings and the miracles Jesus would perform. He prophesied that Jesus would become a great and mighty ruler and that people would rejoice at his birth.

In our day, Jesus has already come to the earth once, but he is going to come again soon. When he comes again, this will be called his Second Coming. The scriptures talk about many signs of his Second Coming.

We read in the scriptures that before Jesus comes again, many good things will happen, but there will also be many bad things like wars and diseases. But we don't have to worry about these bad things because as long as we follow the prophet, Heavenly Father will protect us. Just like the prophets in the scriptures, the prophet today still warns us of danger and helps us to stay righteous.

Thought Question: What things has the prophet told us recently?

2. Jesus Was Born in Bethlehem

Last week Austen's mom went to the hospital to have a baby. After the baby was born, Austen's dad took him to see his new brother. When they reached the nursery, his dad held him up to see the baby better. Austen was so excited to be a big brother to this new little baby.

Just like Austen loved his new brother, we all have a brother who loves us. His name is Jesus. Jesus wasn't born in a hospital. Instead his parents, Mary and Joseph, had to stay in a stable where animals lived. But Mary was so happy when he was born. She wrapped him in cloth. Then she laid Jesus in a manger full of straw, which was used to hold the food for the animals.

It might seem strange that the most important person on earth was born in such a poor place, but Jesus wanted to know what it feels like when we suffer. Because he suffered for you, he always knows how to make you feel better if you come to him.

Thought Question: Do you think Jesus always understands how you feel no matter what?

Scripture

And she brought forth her firstborn son, and wrapped him in swaddling clothes, and laid him in a manger; because there was no room for them in the inn.
—Luke 2:7

Visual Aid:

GAB 30

Illustration Ideas:

A hospital, a new baby, a stable, a manger, baby Jesus, Mary, Joseph

3. Someday Jesus Will Come Again

Scripture

When the Son of man shall come in his glory, and all the holy angels with him, then shall he sit upon the throne of his glory.
—Matthew 25:31

Visual Aid:

GAB 64

Illustration Ideas:

A tree, a lamb, a ring, the Liahona, John, Jesus at the Second Coming

Imagine that you are looking at a tree, a lamb, and a wedding ring. Do you know what these three things have in common? They are all symbols. Almost anything can be a symbol. The scriptures tell us about many symbols. For instance, the Liahona was a symbol to Lehi and his family. It reminded them of how Christ leads us in the right direction. In the book of Revelation, the last book in the Bible, the Apostle John used hundreds of symbols to tell us about one very important event, the Second Coming. The Second Coming is when Christ will return to the earth and reign over us.

When he comes, we will be with him and help him with his work. Through his power, the earth will become even more beautiful and glorious than it is now. No one knows for sure when Jesus will come again, but if we listen to the prophets and do what they tell us, we will be ready for that great day.

Thought Question: Can you name some other symbols in the scriptures and what they symbolize?

4. I Will Be Ready when Jesus Comes

A quail is a type of bird. Quail have a funny way of running instead of flying. When there are lots of quail together in a family, they all run in straight lines. Usually the parents lead and the baby quail follow, making sure they walk in exactly the same direction their parents did.

Heavenly Father wants us to be like quail. Of course, he doesn't want us to run around, making bird noises. But he does want us to follow the good examples around us. He knows that when we do this, we will be safe. Our parents can be good examples just like the quail parents, but we have an even better example to follow. It's the example of our older brother, Jesus Christ.

When we follow Jesus, we will always be safe, no matter what. If we follow his example, we will be ready when he comes again. That will be a great day because we will be able to join Jesus and Heavenly Father and live in their kingdom forever.

Thought Question: What could you do today to prepare for Jesus' Second Coming?

Scripture

And then they shall look for me, and, behold, I will come; and they shall see me in the clouds of heaven, clothed with power and great glory; with all the holy angels; and he that watches not for me shall be cut off.
—D&C 45:44

Visual Aid:

GAB 66

Illustration Ideas:

A family of quail, a pathway, Jesus, the prophet, scriptures, Jesus at the Second Coming

Additional Ideas

_____
_____
_____
_____
_____
_____
_____
_____
_____
_____
_____
_____
_____
_____
_____
_____

Additional Ideas

_____

_____

_____

_____

_____

_____

_____

_____

_____

_____

_____

_____

_____

_____

_____

_____

_____

Additional Ideas

_____
_____
_____
_____
_____
_____
_____
_____
_____
_____
_____
_____
_____
_____
_____
_____

Additional Ideas

_____

_____

_____

_____

_____

_____

_____

_____

_____

_____

_____

_____

_____

_____

_____

_____

Additional Ideas

Additional Ideas

_____

_____

_____

_____

_____

_____

_____

_____

_____

_____

_____

_____

_____

_____

_____

_____

_____

_____

Additional Ideas

Additional Ideas

Additional Ideas

_____

_____

_____

_____

_____

_____

_____

_____

_____

_____

_____

_____

_____

_____

_____

_____

Additional Ideas

About the Author

Heidi Doxey graduated from Brigham Young University. Her favorite part of Primary was always singing time, and she still enjoys singing—mostly as a harmony part to her car stereo.

When she's not writing, Heidi enjoys reading books about punctuation, slowly killing things in her garden, experimenting in the kitchen, and taking road trips to exotic locations like Spanish Fork.